Wild Edible Plants of Arizona

MW00986057

Lincoln Town Press
All rights reserved
Copyright © 2019, 2020 by Charles W. Kane
First edition, Second printing
Library of Congress Control Number: 2019902578
ISBN 10: 099828713X and ISBN 13: 9780998287133

Wild Edible Plants of Arizona is intended solely for educational purposes. The publisher and author disclaim any liability arising from the use of any plant listed in this book.

Printed and bound in the United States of America

Additional Titles by Charles W. Kane
Wild Edible Plants of New Mexico (2019)
Medicinal Plants of the Western Mountain States (2017) · Wild Edible Plants of Texas (2016)
Southern California Food Plants (2013) · Medicinal Plants of the American Southwest (2011)
Sonoran Desert Food Plants (2011/2017) · Herbal Medicine: Trends and Traditions (2009)

Introduction

Within the vast treasury of wild edible plant information, not much mention is given to Arizona's other than desert–lowland vegetation. Wild Edible Plants of Arizona remedies that. With it (and *Sonoran Desert Food Plants*), the plant utilitarian now has an illustrated guide to the most important wild edible plants the state, in its entirety, has to offer.

HIGH ELEVATION MOUNTAINS & PLATEAUS From the San Francisco Peaks and Mogollon Rim to the White Mountains and Sky Islands, Arizona's realm of 7000' and above is limited; however, its dispersement is nearly state–wide (except for the southwest). In some ways, the high elevation areas of Arizona are a southern tapering–off of the Rockies. Conifers and Aspen make up much of the trees overhead, while the understory hosts a bevy of sustaining wild edibles, such as Creeping hollygrape, Dayflower, Serviceberry, and Mountain parsley. The majority of the plants described in *WEPAZ* are found in this zone.

MIDDLE ELEVATION CHAPARRAL & GRASSLAND This expansive section of terrain lies above the desert but below the high mountains. An ecosystem of transition, it exists between quick rain evaporation and snow accumulation, between succulents and tall trees. This region encompasses towns like Sedona, Prescott, Oracle, and Bisbee; in total, possibly a quarter of the state. The edible plant life here tends to be subtle, yet for the observant, bounties are to be found. Emory oak and its mostly trouble–free acorn, Pinyon pine with a nut even gourmets like, and other edibles like Spiderwort and Manzanita, present themselves to the appreciative of the middle–lands.

COURSES OF WATER, PERENNIAL & INTERMITTENT Brought forth by precipitation and shaped by its paths and repositories, water is considered a finite resource in Arizona. But when it coalesces and lingers, the effect that rain and snowmelt has on the wild edible plant milieu is astounding. Arizona dewberry, Yampa, Smartweed, and Yellowdock are just a few plants that not only grow, but need, moistened streamside and/or intermittent drainage–influenced soils to grow and thrive.

What is an edible plant?

Due to the current glut of misleading on–line (and printed) information on the subject, a more involved answer to a seemingly simple question should be presented. First and foremost, let me suggest what an edible plant is not. It is not a medicinal plant (or it's low in this quality). It is not a poisonous plant. Nor is it a plant that provides no sustenance, but still can be chewed and swallowed (in small quantities) without sickness (grass clippings or tree leaves [general], for instance). It is a plant that provides calories and nutrients (vitamins, minerals, etc.) with little to moderate processing. It also is a plant (or a close associate of that plant) that has at least some utilitarian history: if there is no record of indigenous edible use...there's likely a good reason (medicinal/poisonous/no value). If the reader keeps these qualifications in mind, he will be better informed than many edible plant web 'influencers' and related armchair researchers.

Proper Identification

Arizona is home to a significant number of poisonous plants: Water hemlock, Poison hemlock, False hellebore, Tobacco, Coral bean, Monkshood, Datura, and Locoweed are a number of the more significant members. Hundreds more are medicinal/semi–toxic; they are not deadly, but if eaten in meal–quantities, will sicken the forager. Knowing a plant's identity with complete certainty, prior to its gathering and consumption, is a wise practice. Along with this booklet, the use of several field guides (or the instruction of an expert) to confirm identification is optimal in most cases.

Resources & Acknowledgments

I'm a regular user of the SEINet database. To its developers, contributors, and custodians – thank you. My county–by–county locators are largely derivative of the Biota of North America Program site. Concerning classification specifics, I mostly relied upon the Flora of North America (via efloras.org). For a historical indigenous–use perspective, I occasionally referred to Daniel Moerman's Native American Ethnobotany. Jim Verrier was very helpful with his identification clarification of Panicum and Zuloagaea. Appreciated too is Peter Geirlach due to his availability at answering my random classification inquiries.

Poisonous Plants

Note: the plants that should be avoided in Arizona are numerous. The following are a number of the more problematic genera.

Water hemlock (Cicuta)	Water hemlock (Cicuta)	Poison hemlock (Conium)
Poison hemlock (Conium)	Datura	Coral bean (Erythrina)
Tree tobacco (Nicotiana)	Desert tobacco (Nicotiana)	False hellebore (Veratrum)

American Rocket

Barbarea orthoceras

Other Common Names

American wintercress, Erectpod wintercress, Wintercress

Range & Habitat

American rocket enjoys a significant range throughout the West. It's found in all states west of the Continental Divide. In Arizona, it grows between 5000'–10000' and almost always in the moist soils of meadows and streamsides. Look for it from the San Francisco Peaks and Mogollon Rim to the White Mountains and Pinaleños.

Edible Uses

Like others in the Mustard family, American rocket has a pronounced spicy–pungent–mustard taste. The young leaves, flowers, and imma-ture seed pods are consumed fresh, in small amounts, as a salad accent or garnish. Boiled or sautéed briefly, greater quantities can be eaten with-out the occasional irritating qualities of the fresh plant – heat dissipates most of the plant's mustard oils.

Medicinal Uses

Eat a small handful of the fresh leaf if suffering from indigestion (not heart-burn). Many find its stimulating nature re-lieving to gastric stasis and bloating.

Cautions & Special Note

For women, too much of the fresh plant may stimulant menses. Additionally, I've observed large amounts of the fresh plant cause kidney sensitivity and stomach un-ease. The causative principles for this are known as glucosinolates, a group of volatiles common to most Mustard family plants. Small amounts of these compounds are fine; large amounts are irritating. Another mountain/moist–soil growing Mustard found in high elevation Arizona is Bog yellowcress (Rorippa palustris). It too is herbaceous with yellow flowers and elongated seedpods. In terms of edi-bility, it can be treated the same as American rocket.

Sustenance Index: Low
Pictured: *Barbarea orthoceras*

Anoda
Anoda cristata

Other Common Names
Crested anoda, Spurred anoda

Range & Habitat
Found in southern and central parts of the state, look for Anoda throughout middle elevations (3500'–6000'). More of a flat area denizen, rather than that of the mountains, search for the plant in old fields, meadows, and on grassy slopes.

Preferring moist soils, Arizona specimens sprout and develop quickly during the summer rains. Late July through August are the best months to gather the plant.

Edible Uses
Like Mallow (Malva), Anoda belongs to the Mallow family. And like Mallow, Anoda's leaves are picked and eaten as a simple trail–forage. Though a bit hairy, they are pleasant enough to be consumed fresh.

As a spinach–like cooked green, simmer the leaves for 10–15 minutes and serve with butter and seasonings. Like other plants in the Mallow family, once cooked a subtle sliminess may be noticed. This can be eliminated by a quick water rinse prior to serving.

Medicinal Uses & Cautions
A strong leaf infusion is soothing to irritated/inflamed gastrointestinal tissues. The fresh leaf poultice is well applied to minor sun/heat burns and other skin afflictions where redness is a hallmark. There are no cautions for Anoda.

Special Note
Helpful in identification, Anoda's hastate leaves sometimes have blotchy–red mid–veins. This feature is naturally occurring and not the result of a rust/fungal infection.

Sustenance Index: Low
Pictured: *Anoda cristata*

Apache Red Grass
Zuloagaea bulbosa (Panicum bulbosum)

Other Common Names
Bulb panic, Bulb panicgrass

Range & Habitat
A native perennial, Apache red grass is found from Flagstaff and the White Mountains, south to the Pinaleños and Chiricahuas (in fact all the Sky Islands of southeastern Arizona). Elevations of 4000'–8000' potentially host the plant. Look for it on slopes, hillsides, canyon sides and bottoms, and dirt roadsides – all with moist soil.

Edible Uses
Hand–strip the seeds from the panicle in late summer to early fall. Set the seeds aside in a box/paper bag for a week or so. Rub the seeds vigorously to separate the chaff. Winnow the seeds in a light breeze (or fan set on low). Repeat...and repeat again.

Apache red grass is a high–chaff seed – higher than Mexican panicgrass, Indian ricegrass, and Pinyon ricegrass. This means that there will be more processing involved in making it into a worthwhile food. I recommend treating this species as a flour, meal, or gruel base, rather than eating the seed raw (again, lots of chaff).

Medicinal Uses & Cautions
There are no medicinal uses or cautions for Apache red grass.

Special Note
Apache red grass is closely related to Panicgrass. Including this species, there are about half–dozen native Panicgrass species that were once used for food in Arizona. Zuloagaea bulbosa, Panicum hirticaule (Mexican panicgrass), and Panicum capillare (Common panicgrass) were the most commonly employed plants. Due to its regional abundance, it has been suggested that Apache red grass was an Apache wild grain favorite.

Sustenance Index: Medium
Pictured: *Zuloagaea bulbosa*

Arizona Dewberry

Rubus arizonensis

Other Common Names
Arizona blackberry

Range & Habitat
Arizona dewberry is found from Oak Creek Canyon west to Yarnell and south to Patagonia. Although it's most abundant throughout the mountains of the Tonto National Forest, any middle elevation (3500'–5000') shady streamside in the central (and central–southern) part of the state may potentially host the plant.

Arizona dewberry is not exactly prolific, yet where encountered, it's typically abundant. Arizona cypress is a common associate tree.

Edible Uses
Though the fruit size is a little smaller, treat Arizona dewberry like Blackberry in terms of edibility. Sour–sweet (and a bit seedy), the fruit is fine eaten raw, added to snacks once dehydrated, or prepared as a jelly/fruit preserve.

Nutritionally significant, the fruit contains good amounts of vitamin C, potassium, and magnesium.

Medicinal Uses
Use the leaf tea as a mild urinary tract soother. The tea too, internally and externally, can be used as a female postpartum tonic and to generally reduce reproductive tissue irritability.

Cautions & Special Note
There are no cautions for Arizona dewberry.
Occasionally the plant is found growing in a sterile condition. This is mainly due to poor hydration or its existence at too low/high of an elevation. All plants of the Rubus genus are similar in edible (and medicinal) use. Arizona dewberry differs from Blackberry mainly in its size. Blackberry is a big sprawling bush; Arizona dewberry has a smaller and lower–growing profile. Both plants are significantly prickly.

Sustenance Index: Medium
Pictured: *Rubus arizonensis*

Bean, Spotted
Phaseolus maculatus

Other Common Names
Cocolmeca, Metcalf bean, Wild bean

Range & Habitat
Spotted bean is the largest native wild–growing bean found in the state (and possibly in America). It ranges from central and southern Arizona, southwestern New Mexico, West Texas, to Mexico. In Arizona, its greatest densities occur in mid–elevations of the southeastern Sky Islands. Look to slopes, hillsides, and middle valley floors. Manzanita, Oak, and Juniper are common associates.

Edible Uses
After flowering in late summer, the green–immature pods/beans are first to appear. Eat them fresh or boil/roast them as green peas/beans. At this stage they are mild and pleasant–tasting. Further along in the season, gather the almost–dried pod/bean. Allow them to dry fully in a container. Shuck/soak/rinse/boil the dry beans like any other. They are fine tasting and like Tepary in this regard. Nutritious, they contain 20%–30% protein.

Medicinal Uses & Cautions
There are several minor medicinal uses ascribed to Spotted bean (Tarahumara); however, since the plant is on the edge of its range in the Southwest, I recommend leaving the root unmolested. There are no cautions for Spotted bean.

Special Note
Like Tepary, Spotted bean is/was traditionally cultivated/utilized (Mexico) as a food (livestock fodder too). The plant is a large–sprawling perennial vine with erect and very coarse/thickened leaves (three leaflets per leaf). I've observed Tepary and Spotted bean growing side–by–side. Where there is one, the other is likely close by.

Sustenance Index: High
Pictured: *Phaseolus maculatus*

Bean, Tepary

Phaseolus acutifolius

Other Common Names
Wild bean

Range & Habitat

Although wild populations of Tepary have been reported for the upper reaches of the Verde River area, it's most commonly encountered from the Tonto National Forest south throughout the Sky Island ranges of southeastern Arizona. The Pinaleños, Santa Catalinas, Rincons, Chiricahuas, Baboquivaris, Santa Ritas, and Huachucas all have sizable amounts. Once the monsoons arrive in the summer (or after adequate winter rains), keep an eye out for it between 3000'–6000', climbing up through nearby shrubs. Tepary flowers in the late summer and fruits early fall.

Edible Uses

Found in the wild, Tepary is much smaller than domesticated cultivars, but tastes about the same. Pleasant and mild, just be sure to soak, rinse, and simmer the beans until fully cooked. The fresh flowers are not bad tasting. They make a colorful addition to salads and the like.

Indigenous use of Tepary (wild and domesticated), north and south of the border, predates Columbus' arrival to the Americas.

Medicinal Uses, Cautions, & Special Note

There are some minor uses ascribed to the non–bean parts of Tepary; but generally speaking, it's an unremarkable plant in this department.

There are no cautions for Tepary. Tickclover (Desmodium spp.) may be confused with Tepary prior to pod/bean formation. Both plants are vining and have three leaflets per leaf. Wait until pod/bean development to be sure. Tickclover's pods are insignificant compared to Tepary's.

Sustenance Index: High

Pictured: *Phaseolus acutifolius var. tenuifolius*

9

Beeplant

Peritoma serrulata (Cleome serrulata)

Other Common Names
Rocky Mountain beeplant, Bee spiderflower

Range & Habitat
Fairly common throughout the Interior West, in Arizona, Beeplant is found at middle to higher elevations: 5000'–9500'. Disturbed soils such as drainage bottoms/sides, dirt roadsides, and trailsides are several good places to look for the plant. It grows (2'–4' tall) and flowers quickly in response to summer–monsoon rains. It's particularly abundant around Flagstaff.

Edible Uses
The young leaves, flowers, and pods (green/flexible) are gathered mid–summer. Eat these parts fresh (limited) as a spicy/mustard–like salad addition. Better yet, simmer them for 5–10 minutes and rinse with fresh water. Season to taste and eat solo as a cooked green or add Beeplant to other cooked greens as part of a combo.

The young pods (seeds still unformed) are pickled like capers...this will remove much of the pod's natural spiciness. The mature seeds too are edible. They're best soaked, rinsed, dehydrated, ground, and then added in small amounts to other flours.

Medicinal Uses, Cautions, & Special Note
Beeplant is not significantly medicinal, nor are there any cautions for the plant (aside from cautions common to all mustard oil containing plants – see American rocket). The Hopi, Navajo, and Apache utilized Beeplant as an edible due to its abundance and non-toxicity. Clammyweed (Polanisia dodecandra), which belongs to the same family (Cleomaceae), grows lower in elevation, but is smaller and has white flowers (with red stamens). It's occasionally listed as edible. Truth be told, it's sticky, poor–tasting, and more fibrous than Beeplant. Edible, but barely. Like Mustard, Beeplant's spiciness is due to its glucosinolate content.

Sustenance Index: Medium
Pictured: *Peritoma serrulata*

Biscuitroot
Lomatium nevadense

Other Common Names
Nevada biscuitroot, Springparsley, Desert parsley

Range & Habitat
Lomatium nevadense is the widest–ranging and most abundant species of edible Biscuitroot found within the state. Common to foothills and mid–mountains, look to rocky slopes and exposed hillsides between 3000′–7000′.

Edible Uses
Biscuitroot is entirely edible – leaf, stem, seed, and root. The herbaceous portion is best chopped and boiled/sautéed prior to consumption; it's not bad tasting consumed fresh, but it is a little fibrous.

   The thickened and non–woody small roots of Biscuitroot are starchy and bland–tasting, not at all unlike a parsnip. When fresh they can be a little acrid/astringent; however, boiling/cooking or drying/grinding will render them more palatable. They are a good complex carbohydrate source.

Medicinal Uses
Lomatium nevadense (profiled) is not medicinal; however, L. dissectum represents the most common medicinal species of the genus. This species, and any other Lomatium with resinous, balsamic, and bitter–tasting roots, are important lung medicines, especially if there is a viral element affecting the area. The medicinal species of Lomatium tend to be bigger plants with larger roots.

Cautions & Special Note
There are no cautions for Biscuitroot. Springparsley, Mountain parsley, and Biscuitroot (all Carrot family plants) are very similar in growth habit (small herbaceous perennials), edible use, and taste.

Sustenance Index: Medium
Pictured: *Lomatium nevadense*

11

Black Cherry
Prunus serotina var. rufula

Other Common Names
Southwestern black cherry, Black chokecherry, Rum cherry

Range & Habitat
Black cherry in Arizona, New Mexico, and West Texas belongs to variety rufula. In the eastern part of the country, variety serotina is the tree's designation. Aside from minor leaf variations (and tree size), the two varieties are practically identical in appearance (and use).

Mid–mountain elevations, with Juniper, Pinyon, Ponderosa pine, and/or Oak, is Black cherry's most common strata. Usually in proximity to a draw or creek, look for the small tree from Flagstaff and Prescott, south to Sierra Vista and Bisbee. It's common and widespread throughout the state.

Edible Uses
Black cherry fruit is edible fresh, picked directly from the tree. When ripe they are sweet and have a very pleasant cherry (hint of bitter) flavor. Naturally, the pits (seeds) should be spit out before the fruit is eaten (or removed if processing for jelly preparations). Imparting its characteristic flavor, Black cherry fruit mixes very well with other wild berries.

Roast (important) the pits at 350 degrees for 20 minutes or so. Crack the pit (I use a vise) and eat the kernel within. They are small but pleasant and nutty tasting.

Medicinal Uses & Cautions
Dried Black cherry bark is used like Wild cherry (Prunus virginiana) bark: as a standard herbal medicine for a dry cough with bronchial inflammation.

The pits, leaves, and other non–edible parts contain small amounts of toxic cyanogenic glycosides, common to many Rose family plants. Cooking/heating/drying destroys or reduces these compounds.

Sustenance Index: Medium
Pictured: *Prunus serotina var. rufula*

Blackberry
Rubus armeniacus (Rubus discolor, R. procerus)

Other Common Names
Himalayan blackberry

Range & Habitat
The middle elevation mountains of central Arizona host the greatest concentrations of Blackberry: Oak Creek Canyon south through much of Tonto NF. Eurasian in origin, feral populations are almost always centered around old escapee plantings.

Edible uses
When ripe, Blackberry fruit (not an actual berry but a drupe) are dark purple to black, and usually smaller than store–bought. They are sweet, mildly tart, and delicious when gathered from a healthy and well–hydrated specimen.

Eat them raw directly from the plant or prepare them in the form of a jam, jelly, etc. Like other fruits, they can also be dehydrated and reconstituted for use later. Blackberry is a good source of vitamin C and A, magnesium, and health–promoting pigments.

Medicinal uses
Blackberry leaf is a medicinal equivalent to Raspberry leaf, which means the leaf tea is internally used as a mild female reproductive astringent/tonic. Externally, the leaf wash is soothing to tissue redness and inflammation. The root tea is used as a gastrointestinal tract astringent for diarrhea.

Cautions & Special Note
There are no cautions for Blackberry. Most states list this species as an invasive plant. Rubus arizonensis is a native Blackberry (Arizona dewberry). Its range is more limited, but it grows in similar habitats throughout Arizona. Also, even though its fruits are a bit smaller, they are utilized the same as this species.

Sustenance Index: Medium
Pictured: *Rubus armeniacus*

Bracken Fern

Pteridium aquilinum

Other Common Names

Bracken, Western bracken fern

Range & Habitat

Widespread throughout the Northern Hemisphere, Bracken fern enjoys a significant distribution in Arizona. The fern is common to montane locations, usually with Ponderosa pine. In fact, deep pine needle chuff and dappled shade seem to be necessary requirements for its presence.

Edible Uses

Late spring to early summer Bracken fern begins to sprout anew from its sub–surface rhizomes. When the stem shoots are 8"–1' in height, snip them at ground level using clippers (or hands alone are fine). Cover the shoots with fresh water and add a teaspoon of baking soda and a teaspoon of salt. Boil/simmer the shoots for about 15 minutes. Drain, rinse, add fresh water (with baking soda and salt), and simmer again for another ten minutes. Drain, rinse, season, and serve as an asparagus–like vegetable.

Medicinal Uses & Cautions

There are no medicinal uses for Bracken fern. Livestock poisonings (and animal studies) leave no doubt that this fern is a harbinger of carcinogenic, mutagenic, and neurotoxic principles (mainly, ptaquiloside). There is even a correlation between higher esophageal cancer rates and Japanese whom regularly consume Bracken fern. With that said, it is my opinion that eating it (boiled with baking soda and salt – this being a Japanese custom, proven to reduce some of its toxicities) **on occasion** is relatively safe. However, eating the fern regularly is probably not wise. I also advise against children and women while pregnant (or nursing) eating Bracken fern. Additionally, intestinal upset is not uncommon if excess is consumed at any one sitting.

Sustenance Index: Low
Pictured: *Pteridium aquilinum*

14

Chinese Hat
Portulaca umbraticola

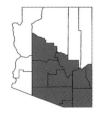

Other Common Names
Wingpod purslane

Range & Habitat
Chinese hat is one of several native Portulaca species found within the state. Common to central and south-eastern Arizona, look for it in disturbed and sandy soils (around draws and on rocky hillsides for instance), between 3000'–6000'.

Edible Uses
The entire above–ground portion is edible. The leaves and stems are succulent and mild tasting, as are the dime–sized five–petaled orange–yellow flowers. Good too are the poppy–like seeds that form later in the summer. They are crunchy and have a mild flavor. All parts are fine consumed fresh, or once briefly sautéed (like bean sprouts).

Medicinal Uses
There are no medicinal uses for Chinese hat.

Cautions
There are no cautions for Chinese hat.

Special Note
The common name Chinese hat is due to the seedpod's resemblance of an Oriental farm/field hat.

A few other Portulaca species are found in Chinese hat's proximity. Similar–appearing Purslane (Portulaca oleracea) occurs throughout Arizona (see Sonoran Desert Food Plants) at a wide array of elevations. Its stem growth is more laterally spreading than Chinese hat's. Shrubby purslane (P. suffrutescens) is often found close by too. This species' leaves are also succulent but narrow and pointed. Edible uses for all Portulaca species are basically interchangeable. These plants contain varying amounts of essential fatty acids, calcium, magnesium, vitamin A, and vitamin C.

Sustenance Index: Low
Pictured: *Portulaca umbraticola*

Creeping Hollygrape

Berberis repens (Berberis aquifolium var. repens, Mahonia repens)

Other Common Names
Creeping mahonia, Little oregongrape, Oregongrape

Range & Habitat
Creeping hollygrape is common to upper–elevation Arizona. Preferring the shade of overhead trees, it's mostly associated with Ponderosa pine (and Gamble oak). Look for this little perennial sub–shrub from 5000' to 8500'. It's also common throughout the greater Rocky Mountain region.

Edible Uses
Ripening from middle to late summer, the small, blue, bloom–covered fruit develop from 6–petaled cup–shaped yellow flowers.

The berries form in clutches and are pleasant tasting: sweet–tart with a hint of bitter. They are fine consumed fresh or can be prepared as a jelly/fruit preserve. Another option is to dehydrate the berries and add them to trail mix and the like.

Medicinal Uses
Creeping hollygrape is a medicinal plant of note. The roots contain significant amounts of isoquinoline alkaloids (berberine, et al.). Useful for an array of liver, gastrointestinal, and microbial complaints, most American herbalists utilize this species (or Berberis aquifolium) in some capacity. See *Medicinal Plants of the Western Mountain States* for a full write–up.

Cautions
There are no cautions for the fruit.

Special Note
Hollygrape (page 28) is used identically to Creeping hollygrape. The main difference being Hollygrape is a large upright shrub; Creeping hollygrape grows to be much smaller in height.

Sustenance Index: Medium
Pictured: *Berberis repens*

Currant
Ribes aureum and R. cereum

Other Common Names
Golden currant, Wax currant

Range & Habitat
Ribes aureum (Golden currant) and R. cereum (Wax currant) are the two main Currant species found in Arizona. Golden currant is located at mid–elevations of 4000'–7000', usually in the moist soils of drainages. From Prescott and Sedona, it is found throughout the central Arizona mountains to ranges of the southeast.

Wax currant grows higher: around 5000'–9000'; look to open forests and with other shrubs on slopes and hillsides. The more abundant of the two species, it is common from north of the Grand Canyon and the San Francisco Peaks to the Mogollon Rim and White Mountains.

Edible Uses
These two species of Currant produce semi–sweet to neutral–tasting berries. They are no award winners for flavor, however, they do make fine jam/jelly candidates. The darker–pigmented Currants, which are not quite as common in Arizona, produce sweeter–tasting fresh berries.

Medicinal Uses
Currant leaves are mildly astringent and used as a fresh poultice for minor scrapes, insect bites, and sunburn.

Cautions
There are no cautious for Currant.

Special Note
Golden currant ripens earlier than Wax currant. Gooseberry (page 25) is another species of Ribes. It has related edible uses, but its fruit is larger and spiky.

Sustenance Index: Medium

Pictured: *Ribes cereum (top & circle)* | *Ribes aureum (bottom)*

Dayflower
Commelina erecta and C. dianthifolia

Other Common Names
Whitemouth dayflower, Birdbill dayflower

Range & Habitat
Commelina erecta is mostly found at middle elevations (grasslands) in southeastern parts of the state.

Commelina dianthifolia, the wider–ranging of the two plants, is common to the mountains around Flagstaff and Prescott, the Mogollon Rim and White Mountains, and south to the Sky Islands.

Edible Uses
All parts of Dayflower are edible. Either raw or cooked, the young growth and upper foliage (especially the flowers and 'pockets' in which they emerge) are a good forage. Pleasant tasting and mild they are non–bitter and can be eaten freely, though the older leaves and stems are often more tough and fibrous.

The roots of Dayflower are fleshy and mild (usually). If found somewhat stringy or marginal–tasting (when soil conditions are dry) a quick water boil and seasoning will help to improve their texture and taste. They don't sit far below the ground's surface so digging is easy. A small trowel is all that is needed.

Medicinal Uses & Cautions
There are no medicinal uses or cautions for Dayflower.

Special Note
The biggest differences between the two species are root and 'pocket' (spathe) shapes. Commelina erecta has fleshy, but non–tuberous roots and compact spathes. C. dianthifolia (Birdbill dayflower) has semi–tuberous roots and spathes with a long and tapering end ('Birdbill').

Sustenance Index: Medium
Pictured: *Commelina dianthifolia (top & bottom)* | *Commelina erecta (circle)*

Elder

Sambucus cerulea (Sambucus glauca, S. neomexicana, S. nigra ssp. cerulea)

Other Common Names
Blue elderberry, Western elder

Range & Habitat
Elder is common to Pine elevations (5000'–8500') throughout the state, but seemingly, only if higher mountains (9000'+) are close by. Another Elder species (Sambucus canadensis or Mexican elder), grows lower in elevation. Its uses are identical to the species profiled here.

Edible Uses
When ripe, Elder berries are blue–black and semi–sweet. Eat them fresh (limited) or dry them for future use. The dried berries can be stored or rehydrated/used as needed. In fact, the drying process concentrates the berries' natural sugars, making them sweeter than fresh. Combine the dried berries with trail mix or eat them as is. The berries are a classic jam/jelly base and can also be fermented instead of grapes to make a wine.

Medicinal Uses & Cautions
The flowers and leaves have similar medicinal uses. Both parts are imbibed as a tea to break a dry fever and as diuretics (the leaves are about twice as strong as the flowers). The tea is also used as a low–level antiviral during the cold and flu season. Elderberry syrup has a modern following as a cold and flu remedy – this is a recent application with no historical or traditional precedent. If sick, use the flower (or leaf) tea for therapeutic results. Use El-

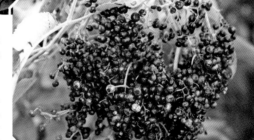

derberry syrup – on pancakes. The seeds (and other parts of Elder) contain small amounts of sambucine and cyanogenic glycosides. Although these compounds are toxic in larger amounts, eating a small handful of the fresh fruit (with the seed) is not a problem. For the ingestion of larger quantities, the fruit should be heated/dried (which destroys/reduces these compounds) and/or strained of their small seeds (jelly bag).

Sustenance Index: Medium
Pictured: *Sambucus cerulea*

19

Emory Oak

Quercus emoryi

Other Common Names
Bellota, Black oak

Range & Habitat
Look for Emory oak from Sedona, Prescott, and Payson, south to Patagonia, and east to Portal (and southeastern NM). It's associated with middle mountains, grassland, Pinyon, and Juniper; it's common and abundant.

Edible Uses
Emory oak acorns are unique because they only occasionally need leaching and when they do, their treatment will be less than other species. Once ripe (fall) gather them by branch shaking or from the ground (recent). Only acorns with no worm/insect holes and w/o damaged shells should be selected. Lay them out to dry – 1–2 weeks (optional). Crack the shell and eat the acorn! There should be little to no astringency and only a hint of bitter (not overpowering). Eat them alone as a snack or chopped and mixed with trail mix/nuts. As a sweet treat the shelled acorns can be prepared as a candied nut. To consume larger amounts, even Emory oak should be leached; however, the number of leaching rounds will be less than with other species. Pulverize the acorns; cover with water; when the water becomes discolored, strain and rinse; repeat until water is clear (or almost clear). Thoroughly leached meal should be neutral tasting. The meal can be prepared as a gruel, shaped (mixed with maple syrup or honey) and dried as a cake, or dried completely and mixed with other flours in baking.

Medicinal Uses & Cautions
Oak bark (tannins) topically reduces tissue redness and irritation. The bark tea is imbibed as a counter for diarrhea; however, large amounts of the tea may cause constipation and kidney irritation (tannins). There are no cautions for acorns (possible constipation if eaten in excess).

Sustenance Index: High
Pictured: *Quercus emoryi*

Evening Primrose, Hooker's

Oenothera elata ssp. hirsutissima (Oenothera hookeri)

Other Common Names
Evening primrose, Western evening primrose

Range & Habitat
Hooker's evening primrose grows at about 5000'–9500' throughout much of Arizona. Almost always found in disturbed soils, roadsides are one of its preferred habitats, though sandy/loamy creek beds and intermittent drainages will be better places to look for uncontaminated plants.

Edible Uses
Late first year or early second year roots (the plant is a biannual) are best for edible uses. Be sure to gather the root when the plant is still a basal rosette of leaves, before it develops a stalk; otherwise the roots will be too woody to utilize. Discard the leaves and chop and boil the roots for 15 minutes (or longer). Drain, rinse, season, and then serve as a vegetable of sorts. The taste is fair, but the texture is somewhat fibrous.

The seeds, garbled from the dried pods, can be ground and eaten or sprinkled on salads and the like for their nutritional aspects.

Medicinal Uses
If nothing else is available, use the fresh poulticed herb on rashes, insect bites, and sunburn. It is mildly soothing. The seeds (Oenothera biennis) are a main source for gamma linolenic acid (consider Hooker's evening primrose to be similar). Deficiency of this essential fatty acid has been linked to glandular and inflammatory problems.

Cautions & Special Note
There are no cautions for the plant. Oenothera biennis' (very similar to this species) roots were once used in war–torn parts of Europe as a famine food, mostly as a soup ingredient.

Sustenance Index: Medium
Pictured: *Oenothera elata ssp. hirsutissima*

Fairybells

Prosartes trachycarpa (Disporum trachycarpum)

Other Common Names

Rough–fruited fairy–bells, Rough–fruited mandarin

Range & Habitat

Fairybells tends to grow between 5500'–10000' as an understory herbaceous perennial. Commonly found in the shaded and moist soils of coniferous forests, look for it from northern Arizona and the Mogollon Rim to the White Mountains and a number of the Sky Island chains of the southeast. The plant is widespread but occasional in population density.

Edible Uses

Eat the fruit of Fairybells when immature. They are most appealing prior to ripening. At this point they are greenish–white and taste pleasant and cucumber–like. If allowed to fully ripen (reddish–orange) they become poortasting and mushy. Fairybells' best use is as a simple trail snack when encountered.

Medicinal Uses

I am unfamiliar with any medicinal use for Fairybells.

Cautions

There are no cautions for Fairybells.

Special Note

Two similar–appearing plants are often found along with Fairybells. Neither are poisonous; however, I cannot fully attest to their palatability.

False Solomon's Seal (Maianthemum racemosum) develops a red berry, but I have found it to be sweet–bitter and unpalatable. Star Solomon's Seal (Maianthemum stellatum) has a green (with blue stripes) berry when immature that turns black when ripe. I have yet to sample Star Solomon's Seal, so am unable to offer an opinion.

Sustenance Index: Medium
Pictured: *Prosartes trachycarpa*

False Virginia Creeper

Parthenocissus vitacea

Other Common Names
Woodbine, Thicket creeper

Range & Habitat
False Virginia creeper is somewhat common in Arizona, growing in the northern/central/southeastern mountains at middle elevations of 4000'–7000'. Look for the plant in creek beds, canyon bottoms, and similar sites where the ground holds more moisture than surrounding areas. It's a vining plant, and almost always found traipsing up through support shrubs and trees.

Edible Uses
The edible part of False Virginia creeper is not the fruit (I repeat, not the fruit), but rather the very young leafing vine tips. Snip them from the plant when they first emerge in the spring and eat fresh or prepare them as a cooked green. Mild and pleas-ant–tasting, they need little if any processing.

Medicinal Uses
There are no significant medicinal uses for False Virginia creeper.

Cautions
Do not eat the fruit! They are very acrid, and if chewed and swallowed, will irritate and inflame the mouth, throat, and stom-ach. If the young leaves are found acrid, it usually means it's too late in the season and they are too mature to eat without mouth/throat irritation.

Special Note
False Virginia creeper and Wild grape belong to same family: Vitaceae. Aside from a few minor differences (tendrils and flowers), False Virginia creeper should be considered identical in use and appearance to the easterly–growing Virginia creeper (Parthenocissus quinquefolia).

Sustenance Index: Low
Pictured: *Parthenocissus vitacea*

Fendler's Sedge

Cyperus fendlerianus

Other Common Names
Fendler's flatsedge, Fendler's nutgrass

Range & Habitat
Fendler's sedge is found state–wide throughout Arizona's upper–middle (5000'–7300') elevations. Preferring soils drier than most other Sedge species and almost always associated with open Ponderosa pine forests, look for it around draws, openings, meadows, soil banks, and old dirt roadsides/cuts.

Edible Uses
While most Sedge species are list-ed as being semi–edible, Fendler's sedge is one of the group's higher–ranking species in this department.

    Each stem is anchored by a shal-low cluster of fibrous roots. Attached to the small root crown are one to sev-eral (usually) corn–kernel sized bulb-lets (I call them niblets). These starchy and mild–sweet tasting pieces are fine consumed raw – after cleaning them up a little by scraping off their external–brown protective layer. For more than a small handful, they'll be easier to digest if first mashed and simmered in water for 20-30 minutes.

Medicinal Uses & Cautions
There are no medicinal uses or cautions for Fendler's sedge.

Special Note
Fendler's sedge (like most Sedges) has three–angled stems and three (sometimes two) leaves per bunch. Yellow nutsedge (Cyperus esculentus var. leptostachyus) is another root–food Sedge species. It's found in moister soils and is smaller in stature, with a more spreading/less compact flower/seedhead. Its small ovoid tubers are attached to fibrous roots away from the root crown.

Sustenance Index: Medium
Pictured: *Cyperus fendlerianus*

Gooseberry

Ribes pinetorum

Other Common Names
Orange gooseberry

Range & Habitat
From 7000'–10000', look for Gooseberry in open coniferous forests and along forest edges. It grows from northern Arizona and Flagstaff to the White Mountains and Sky Islands of southeastern parts of the state.

Edible Uses
Gooseberries are the size of a small grape and dark red/purple when fully ripe. They are only mildly sweet (like Currant); however, the fruit's bristles are its main concern when consumed fresh. I recommend placing the berry carefully between the teeth (molars) and slowly chew one at a time to break the spiky bristles; then swallow normally.

Gooseberries too make a fine jelly base or can be dried and rehydrated for future use. Additionally, like most Ribes berries, Gooseberry is high in vitamin C.

Medicinal Uses
Like Currant leaves, Gooseberry leaf is a mild astringent and can be used as a topical soother for minor sunburn, scrapes, and abrasions.

Cautions
There are no cautions for Gooseberry.

Special Note
In Arizona, with one exception (Gooseberry currant/Ribes montigenum, which is a Currant–type with thorns), all Ribes species can be separated into one of two groups by whether they have stem/node thorns. If the plant is spiny, then it is a Gooseberry. If the plant is spineless, then it is a Currant. Aside from slight botanical differences, edible (and medicinal) uses for both types are the same.

Sustenance Index: Medium
Pictured: *Ribes pinetorum*

Greenthread

Thelesperma megapotamicum

Other Common Names
Cota, Hopi tea, Indian tea, Navajo tea, Pampa tea

Range & Habitat
Considered the most prolific–grower of the Thelesperma genus, look for Greenthread at middle elevations (up to about 9000'). It's most abundant to the east of the north–south axis of Page–Flagstaff–Tucson. Sandy soils of dirt roadsides, flats, and slopes are some typical places to look for the plant.

Edible Uses
Greenthread is a traditional Hopi and Navajo tea plant. Not particularly medicinal, the herbal infusion is simply imbibed as a pleasant–tasting beverage. Mild and non–bitter, the tea can be sipped alone, or mixed with other herbs as part of a combination.

Not a well–known use: the very young leaves, when first emerging from the ground, before stem development, are gathered and chopped, and added fresh to salads and the like as an accent/garnish.

Medicinal Uses
Greenthread is a mild diuretic.

Cautions
There are no cautions for Greenthread.

Special Note
The foliage and roots were once processed to form a yellow–brown pigment. Other species of Greenthread are also found in Arizona; Thelesperma subnudum or Navajo tea (northern Arizona) and T. longipes or Longstalk greenthread (southeastern AZ) are somewhat common in their regional abodes. They too can be used like Greenthread.

Sustenance Index: Low
Pictured: *Thelesperma megapotamicum (top & bottom)* | *Thelesperma longipes (circle)*

Hog Potato
Hoffmannseggia glauca (Hoffmannseggia drepanocarpa)

Other Common Names
Indian rushpea, Waxy rushpea, Pignut, Tater of the hog

Range & Habitat
A common small perennial of the Southwest, Hog potato is found at lower elevations, up to about 5000'. It prefers the disturbed–sandy soils of dirt roadsides, feral fields, and wash/intermittent drainage sides. It's mostly found south of I–40. Plentiful stands additionally exist in southern California, New Mexico, and Texas.

Edible Uses
A vexing edible plant, it's the small potato–like tuber that is the sought–after part. Attached to long and thin rhizomes from the foliage above, they lie 2'–3' below the ground's surface. However, even the most careful and patient digger may come away empty–handed, as the rhizomes don't always seem to lead to tubers (the age of the colony may be a factor).

My greatest success with gathering Hog potato has been simply picking the tubers up from drainage sides after a forceful summer rain – the rushing rainwater cuts into the ground, exposing the tubers, making their collection effortless.

The tubers are really too tough to be eaten raw. They should first be cooked (chopped and boiled or wrapped in foil and baked). Once cooked, they are pleasant and distinctly potato–like in texture and taste.

Medicinal Uses, Cautions, & Special Note
There are no medicinal uses or cautions for Hog potato. It's said that swine seek out the tuber if the plant is in their proximity.

Sustenance Index: High
Pictured: *Hoffmannseggia glauca*

Hollygrape

Berberis fremontii (Mahonia fremontii) and B. haematocarpa (M. haema-tocarpa)

Other Common Names
Fremont's barberry, Fremont's mahonia, Red barberry, Red mahonia

Range & Habitat
Berberis fremontii is found through-out central and northern parts of the state, to about 7000'. B. haema-tocarpa is found state–wide, but at slightly lower elevations. Look for ei-ther shrub in chaparral zones – with Juniper, Pinyon, and Oak (and/or Mesquite for B. haematocarpa). Both plants are common, and in some en-virons, cover vast tracks of land.

The two species are not easy to tell apart. Berberis fremontii's termi-nal leaflet is wider then B. haemato-carpa's elongated leaflet. Other char-acteristics (and edibility) are basically identical.

Edible Uses
A summertime berry, Hollygrape's fruit are edible raw. They are a unique combination of sweet, tart, and slightly bitter – not at all unpleasant. Dry the berries (insignificant seeds) for a snack or trail mix addition. As a jelly base, they are equally fine.

Medicinal Uses & Cautions
Medicinal uses (root) for Hollygrape are identical to Creeping hollygrape. For these purposes I prefer Creeping hollygrape...it's a lot easier to gather. There are no cautions for the fruit.

Special Note
Scientific names for this group of plants can be trying. The old system was simple and made this distinction: if the plant has holly–like spiny leaves, it's a Mahonia (Hollygrape, Oregon-grape, etc.); however, if the plant has stem and branch thorns, it's a Berberis (Barberry). Now though, classifiers lump them all in the Berberis genus. Fortunately, for edible and medicinal purposes, both plants, spiny–leaved or thorny shrub, are used the same.

Sustenance Index: Medium
Pictured: *Berberis fremontii*

Jones' Beeplant
Peritoma jonesii (Cleome lutea var. jonesii)

Other Common Names
Jones' spiderflower

Range & Habitat
Jones' beeplant is found throughout much of the state; however, it is most abundant in two areas: central and southern Arizona. Look to middle elevation floodplains, such as the Verde River Valley and southern reaches of the Santa Cruz River. It's a quick grower (annual) in response to monsoon rains and is almost always found in moist soils with water close by.

Edible Uses
Mustard–like in taste (like others of the Peritoma/Cleome genera) the young foliage, flowers, and green pods are eaten fresh as a garnish or salad ingredient. Larger amounts can be consumed once sautéed or boiled. Mix Jones' beeplant with other greens as a mustard–like addition to stir–frys. Like capers, the green pods and unopened flower buds can be pickled in a vinegar brine. The mature seeds too are edible. They're best soaked, rinsed, dehydrated, ground, and then added in small amounts to other flours. The Bee plant (Cleomaceae) and Mustard (Brassicaceae) families are closely related and share several chemical characteristics; one being, glucosinolates (Mustard oil), which is responsible for these plant's pungent–spicy tastes.

Medicinal Uses
The Navajo ritually employed this species and used it in some capacity as a topical treatment for insect bites.

Cautions
A small handful of the fresh leaf (chewed and swallowed) is useful in relieving indigestion – but too much may cause heartburn.

Sustenance Index: Low
Pictured: *Peritoma jonesii*

Madrone
Arbutus arizonica

Other Common Names
Arizona madrone, Madroño

Range & Habitat
Madrone is a small to medium sized tree found throughout the middle elevations of southeastern Arizona. Often intermingled with Oak and Pinyon pine, it's common to the Santa Catalinas, Santa Ritas, Chiricahuas, Pinaleños, and Huachucas.

Edible Uses
Madrone berries are a fair edible. They are better tasting than Manzanita berries but not quite as good as Blueberries (all Heath family plants). In years of poor rainfall, they can be a bit mealy and only mildly sweet, but still, it's a worthwhile plant to know, regardless of high or low precipitation.

Eat the fruit raw, or once dried, sprinkle them into trail mix and other snacks. As a jam or jelly base, the fruit excels, and this may be Madrone's best utilization.

Medicinal Uses
Madrone leaf tea is used as a urinary tract disinfectant. It will be found milder than Uva–ursi or Manzanita leaf tea, two related plants with similar medicinal properties.

Cautions
There are no cautions for the fruit.

Special Note
The fruit of Arbutus arizonica is likely similar in nutritional content to the Mediterranean species, A. unedo. It's used locally as the base material for an alcohol beverage (in Greece, known as Koumaro). Vitamins C and E, carotenoids, anthocyanins/anthocyanidins and other phenols, non–volatile acids (malic, citric, etc.) and sugars are reported for its fruit.

Sustenance Index: Medium
Pictured: *Arbutus arizonica*

Manzanita
Arctostaphylos pungens and *A. pringlei*

Other Common Names
Pointleaf manzanita, Pringle's manzanita

Range & Habitat
Arctostaphylos pungens and A. pringlei are the two most prevalent Manzanita species in Arizona. A. pungens (Pointleaf manzanita) has a slightly greater distribution; however, both species are found at middle elevations throughout the state. A common plant, look to zones above the desert but below the Pines.

Edible Uses
Like the fruit of most (if not all) other Heath family plants, Manzanita is edible. Sweet (but mealy, semi–astringent, and seed–filled) the fruit has a distinct apple–like flavor (Manzanita is Spanish for 'little apple'). They can be eaten freely when encountered, but by far their best use is as a jelly base. Animals relish the fruit and they are a favorite of bears.

Medicinal Uses
The leaf tea is a popular regional herbal treatment for urinary tract infections. It is an analog to Uva–ursi (Arctostaphylos uva–ursi), a better–known Heath family plant also used for similar problems.

Cautions
There are no cautions for Manzanita fruit consumption.

Special Note
Most species of Manzanita have a very distinctive smooth, reddish–brown outward bark layer. The flowers are urn–shaped and form in hanging groups. Silk tassel (Garrya spp.) may be confused with Manzanita when not in season. Silk tassel's fruit are purple–black and are non–edible. Manzanita is related to Madrone in edible/medicinal use. The two are of the same family.

Sustenance Index: Medium
Pictured: *Arctostaphylos pungens*

Mountain Parsley
Pseudocymopterus montanus (Cymopterus lemmonii)

Other Common Names
Alpine false springparsley

Range & Habitat
Essentially a Rocky Mountain plant that thrives equally well throughout the high mountains of Arizona, look for Mountain parsley from the Kaibab Plateau, south through the San Francisco Peaks, Mogollon Rim, White Mountains, to the Sky Islands of southeastern parts of the state. Mostly associated with Pine, it's a common plant at 7000'–8000' and higher.

Edible Uses
Consider Mountain parsley an important wild edible to know in the Arizona mountains. The entire plant is edible and since the roots are the main part, it provides more sustenance than many other plants.

　　The roots: tender taproots that shred easily, they usually are unbranched and reach depths of 1'–2'. Eat them fresh or chop and cook as needed. The above–ground foliage is also edible. Eat these parts fresh or cooked. All parts have an agreeable fresh–mild parsley taste/smell.

Medicinal Uses & Cautions
There are no medicinal uses or cautions.

Special Note
Two deadly plants, Poison hemlock (PH) and Water hemlock (WH) are related to Mountain parsley (MP). Here are some important differences: leaflet veins of WH travel to the cut (between teeth). Veins of MP travel to the tip. WH grows in or on the edge of water. MP does not. WH and PH are much larger than MP (only 1'–2'). PH prefers moist and disturbed soils. MP prefers drier and better–established soils. PH grows lower (usually) in elevation than MP. If still in doubt, wait for MP to flower: WH and PH have white flowers; MP has yellow, or sometimes red–orange flowers.

Sustenance Index: Medium
Pictured: *Pseudocymopterus montanus*

32

Mullein
Verbascum thapsus

Other Common Names
Woolly mullein, Gordolobo

Range & Habitat
Mullein is a biannual, non–native (Europe) weed. Exceedingly common to Ponderosa pine elevations, it's found almost always in disturbed soils – roadsides, trailsides, and fire–swept areas.

Edible Uses
Select a second–year plant in early to mid–summer. Clip the last 8"–12" of flexible flowering stalk and carefully remove the adhering flower buds and outer rough layer. What's left will be a tender and pliable inner stem, somewhat thinner than a pencil.

The inner stem is eaten raw or cooked and seasoned. It has an asparagus–like taste and texture which lends it to being used as a dish alone or in combination with other wild foods. Given that entire mountain sides (after a fire) are often covered by hundreds of plants, Mullein is an often over–looked but very abundant wild food that takes only a small amount of effort to process.

Medicinal Uses
Mullein leaf is a standard herbal treatment for a dry hacky cough. The root is used for urinary irritations, and the flower, prepared as an oil, is a soothing earache treatment.

Cautions
There are no cautions for Mullein.

Special Note
Mullein is occasionally referred to as 'Toilet–paper plant' by campers due to its leaf size and softness. Proceed at your own risk...itchy!

Sustenance Index: Medium
Pictured: *Verbascum thapsus*

Nettle

Urtica dioica ssp. gracilis and U. gracilenta

Other Common Names
Stinging nettle, California nettle, Mountain nettle

Range & Habitat
Urtica dioica ssp. gracilis (perennial) is the most abundant Nettle species throughout Arizona. It is common to streamsides, intermittent drainages, and similar moist and shady areas. From northern Arizona to the White Mountains and Pinaleños, look for it at elevations of 3500'–9000' (usually 6000'–9000'). Urtica gracilenta (annual) or Mountain nettle is relegated to southeastern Arizona. For this species look to middle elevations, usually between 4000'–6000'. It too prefers moist and shady areas.

Edible Uses
The ideal time to gather Nettle is when it is young and first forming in the spring, prior to the plant becoming fibrous and coarse. It is important to simmer/boil Nettle for 5–10 minutes, sometimes longer depending on the coarseness/age of the plant. This will soften the herb and render the stinging hairs inert (see Cautions). Once boiled, Nettle has the consistency of most other cooked wild greens. They are non–bitter and nutrient–rich.

Medicinal Uses, Cautions, & Special Note
Drink the leaf tea as a mineral–rich and alkalizing beverage. The tea is also soothing to urinary irritations and calming to rhinitis/hayfever. Wear gloves/long sleeves when collecting Nettle due to its stinging hairs (trichomes). If stung, the weal (welt) subsides in 30–60 minutes; nevertheless, it is mildly to moderately painful. If Nettle greens are not cooked sufficiently some mouth/throat irritation may occur from improperly neutralized trichomes contacting oral tissues. Prior to Cotton's dominance, Nettle's fibrous stems (like Hemp) were once a base material for cloths, tents, bags, etc.

Sustenance Index: Low
Pictured: *Urtica dioica ssp. gracilis (top)* | *Urtica gracilenta (bottom)*

New Mexico Raspberry
Rubus neomexicanus

Other Common Names
New Mexico thimbleberry

Range & Habitat
Forested canyon sides, slopes, and draw edges are common places to look for this large shrub. Even though the plant's name refers to New Mexico, its greatest numbers occur in Arizona. Higher points throughout the Colorado Plateau, along Oak Creek Canyon and the Mogollon Rim, and the Sky Islands of southeastern parts of the state, are some of the plant's usual locales.

Edible Uses
Closely related to Raspberry and Thimbleberry, New Mexico raspberry is only fair tasting when ripe. The drupelets are small compared to its large drupe core, which makes them only semi–sweet and dry/mealy when consumed fresh. They also have a peculiar artificial–sweet flavor. Alone or in combination with other fruits, the berry's best use is as a jelly base. Of all the Rubus species, this one is my least favorite.

Medicinal Uses
Containing flavonoids and tannins, the leaf tea is used as a replacement for Raspberry. In other words, use it as a urinary and female reproductive astringent.

Cautions
There are no cautions for New Mexico raspberry.

Special Note
Like Thimbleberry, New Mexico raspberry has no thorns. All other Rubus species in Arizona are armed: Blackberry, Dewberry, and Raspberry.

Sustenance Index: Low
Pictured: Rubus neomexicanus

Ox–Eye Daisy
Leucanthemum vulgare

Other Common Names
Great ox–eye, Field daisy, Maudlin daisy

Range & Habitat
An isolated yet abundant non–native plant, Ox–eye daisy grows from the White Mountains and Mogollon Rim to Flagstaff and the Kaibab Plateau. Look to dirt roadsides, open meadows, and forest edges with full sun exposures.

Edible Uses
Gather the basal leaves early in the season before the plant develops a flowering stalk. At this point in time they will be slightly thickened and tender. Fresh, they have a mild taste and are fine used as a garnish or salad addition. Larger amounts should be boiled/sautéed and seasoned accordingly.

Medicinal Uses
The dried upper herb (flower and leaf), prepared as a tea is a mild child–safe sudorific/sedative, similar to Chamomile in effect.

Cautions
There are no cautions for Ox–eye daily.

Special Note
A number of other Leucanthemum/Chrysanthemum species (i.e Chrysanthemum cinerariaefolium or Dalmatian daisy) contain pyrethrins, a group of naturally occurring compounds with well–documented insecticidal properties. These compounds also tend to be mildly to moderately toxic when ingested in sufficient quantities. There are no consistent reports of Ox–eye daisy containing these compounds, at least in greater than trace amounts.

Sustenance Index: Low
Pictured: *Leucanthemum vulgare*

Panicgrass, Mexican
Panicum hirticaule

Other Common Names
Mexican witchgrass, Roughstalk witchgrass

Range & Habitat
Mexican panicgrass is a native annual, found principally in Arizona and southwestern New Mexico (and Mexico to South America). It's abundant at all elevations up to 7000'. Common to a surprising array of habitats (washsides and bottomlands to open hillsides and slopes), its main determining factor is soil moisture from summer rains. With a good monsoon season, entire gulches may be covered by the grass (August). It can be elusive to find at first; but once a population is located, its abundance is often surprising.

Edible Uses
Snip the entire panicle (with 2"–3" of stem) from the grass in late August – too soon and the seeds will not be mature; too late and they will have fallen. Place the panicles in a paper bag and set them aside for about a week. Strip the seeds from the stems by pinching low on the bunch and pulling towards the top. And/or the panicles can be rolled between the hands. Give the seeds (and small stems) a vigorous hand–rubbing and then winnow them in a light breeze (or fan on low). Compared to Indian ricegrass, the seeds are easy to process (but much smaller). Enjoy the whole seed (crunchy–mildly nutty) solo, or sprinkled on salads, meat, etc. They too are fine for flour/meal/gruel/sun–dried cakes. Nutritious, they contain good amounts of protein, carbohydrates, and fats.

Medicinal Uses, Cautions, & Special Note
There are no medicinal uses or cautions for Mexican panicgrass. Like most Panicum species, this plant provided an important nutritional source in primitive times.

Sustenance Index: High
Pictured: *Panicum hirticaule*

Pinyon Pine

Pinus cembroides, P. edulis, and P. monophylla

Other Common Names

Mexican pinyon, Two–needle pinyon, Single–leaf pinyon

Range & Habitat

These short–stocky pine trees either have one needle (P. monophylla), two needles (P. edulis), or three needles (P. cembroides) per bunch. They are common to the mid–mountains, just below Ponderosa pine elevations.

Edible Uses

Pinyon pines' seeds (or 'nuts') are larger than other Pine species, which makes them a worthwhile wild food. During the summer, when they are still green, throw the cones in a campfire (or use a barbecue grill/ large wok). Once expanded by heat, remove the green cones from the fire. Let them cool a little and remove the seeds. Tear away the thin shell (it should be pliable at this point) and eat the fresh inner seed.

In the late summer–early fall remove the mature seeds from the cone. Use a nut cracker or a gentle hammer tap to crack the shell. Consume the seed freely.

Pinyon pine seeds are very nutritious, fine–tasting, and need no preparation, aside from shelling. They are the wild American version of European pine nuts found in commerce.

Medicinal Uses, Cautions, & Special Note

Pine pitch (Pine sap) is antibacterial and can be used internally (as a tincture) for bronchial, urinary, and intestinal infections or used topically (diluted) for skin infections. Pine needles and inner bark contain small amounts of vitamin C. An infusion of the dried green needles makes a good cold and flu tea.

Applied topically (undiluted), Pine pitch is a tissue irritant (and is flammable). The pitch also can be used as a primitive patching material and sealant.

Sustenance Index: High
Pictured: *Pinus cembroides*

Plantain
Plantago major

Other Common Names
Common plantain, Lanté

Range & Habitat
Plantain is a non–native short–lived perennial. Absent from drier desert regions, look for the plant in moist disturbed soils such as trailsides, meadows, and streamsides (and even untended lawns). Generally abundant at elevations of 5000'–7000', it's a plant that is encountered with little searching.

Edible Uses
Plantain is entirely edible, yet the young springtime leaves are the choice part. They can be eaten fresh, but most find them better as a cooked green. Sautéed, boiled, or steamed, the leaves are fair–tasting and can be eaten alone, or added to other wild food preparations.

Medicinal Uses
A mild plant medicine, Plantain is simply used topically as a soothing vulnerary. Internally, as a tea or fresh juice, it is antiinflammatory and healing to gastrointestinal ulcerations.

Cautions
There are no cautions for Plantain.

Special Note
All other species of Plantain are edible (or at least not poisonous), though this species is considered one of the best in Arizona. Psyllium fiber, a common over–the–counter dietary supplement, is derived from the seed/seed husk of Plantago ovata. Plantain is unrelated to the cooking type of plantain (Musa spp.). The latter is a type of banana that is often used in Mexican cuisine.

Sustenance Index: Low
Pictured: *Plantago major*

Raspberry
Rubus idaeus ssp. strigosus

Other Common Names
Red raspberry, American red raspberry, Western red raspberry

Range & Habitat
A common Rocky Mountain grower, Raspberry is abundant throughout Arizona's higher mountain elevations. Look for the plant from the Kaibab Plateau and San Francisco Peaks, to the White Mountains and southeastern Sky Island ranges. It's most often found along forest openings, trailsides, and other similarly exposed places.

Edible Uses
Found in the wild, Raspberry fruit tends to be a little smaller than store–bought cultivars; however, at peak ripeness they are just as sweet, possibly even more–so. They are fine consumed fresh and can too be utilized as a preserve or jelly base. In all ways, consider wild Raspberry identical in use to the fruit found in commerce.

Raspberry fruit is relatively high in vitamin C, containing approximately 30 mg. per 8 ounces. It also is a fair source of several B vitamins and vitamin E.

Medicinal Uses
Raspberry leaf tea is a female reproductive tonic mainly used during the last trimester of pregnancy. The tea is also soothing to urinary tract irritation.

Cautions & Special Note
There are no cautions for the plant. Raspberry is closely related to New Mexico raspberry, Blackberry, Arizona blackberry, and Thimbleberry (all Rubus species). Most cultivars are derived from European raspberry (Rubus idaeus ssp. idaeus). The leaf underside of Raspberry is nearly white.

Sustenance Index: Medium
Pictured: *Rubus idaeus ssp. strigosus*

Redbud
Cercis occidentalis

Other Common Names
Western redbud, Southwestern redbud

Range and Habitat
A native small tree, Redbud is most populous in California. However, if fortunate enough to be meandering within Havasu and Kanab Canyons, the Grand Canyon, and related terrain further to the east, look for Redbud on the sides of primary and secondary drainages. Additionally, the occasional specimen is found in the Superstitions, Sierra Ancha, and sporadically throughout the Tonto National Forest.

Edible Uses
Developing before the leaves in the spring, the flowers are eaten as is or mixed with other foods as an accent. They are pleasant tasting with a hint of nectar sweetness. The immature pods (and still forming beans) are gathered several weeks later and prepared and eaten just like garden pea–pods. They can be eaten raw, however, they're a little astringent. They are much better seasoned after a quick boil and water rinse. Once cooked, they even have a hint of lemony tang. As the season progresses and the pods become fibrous and dry, it is now time to collect the mature beans. Allow the pods to fully dry in a bucket. Once dried, hand–crush the pods in order to release the beans. Discard the crushed pod parts and cook the dried beans of Redbud like any other. They are significantly smaller than a red or pinto bean, but about the same in nutritional value. Be sure to soak them overnight (and replace the water) before cooking them completely. They may need a second/third rinse when half cooked to remove any lingering poor flavor.

Medicinal Uses and Cautions
Redbud (leaf/bark) was once used as a simple astringent. There are no cautions for Redbud.

Sustenance Index: High
Pictured: *Cercis occidentalis*

Ricegrass, Indian

Achnatherum hymenoides (Oryzopsis hymenoides)

Other Common Names

Indian mountain ricegrass, Indian millet, Silky mountain rice

Range & Habitat

A native bunch–grass common to the Mountain West, in Arizona, Indian ricegrass is concentrated in the northern part of the state, particularly on the high plateaus (Colorado/Kaibab). Foragers looking south of Prescott–Sedona–Mogollon Rim will likely be disappointed. From 3500'– 6500' on flats, basins, mesas, and drainage sides, all with well–drained/ dry soils, are the plant's usual places.

Edible Uses

The seed is gathered from late spring through early fall – lower elevation plants flower/fruit earlier than higher elevation ones. Lightly pinch with thumb and forefinger below a fruiting panicle; then gently pull, stripping the seed away from the stem. Place the seed in a paper bag and repeat. Set the seed aside for 1–2 weeks so it dries completely. One de–chaffing technique for small amounts is to simply rub a bunch between hands several feet above a container in a light breeze (or a fan set on low). Slowly let the seed/ chaff fall. The breeze will take away the chaff while the heavier seed drops into the container. Keep repeating this process until only the grain remains. Another way is to parch the seed, so the fuzzy chaff is burnt away (bottom photo). Prepare Indian ricegrass like any other seed/grain: cooked whole, as a flour or meal, etc.

Medicinal Uses, Cautions, & Special Note

There are no medicinal uses/cautions for Indian ricegrass. Before corn arrived on the scene, the plant was a main grain staple of the western Indians. The plant's commonality and seed size (for a native grass, it's one of the largest) made it a valuable and much utilized edible.

Sustenance Index: High
Pictured: *Achnatherum hymenoides*

Ricegrass, Pinyon
Piptochaetium fimbriatum

Other Common Names
Pinyon speargrass

Range & Habitat
Primarily a southeastern Arizona/ southwestern New Mexico (and Mexico) native species, look for Pinyon ricegrass at middle mountain elevations (5000'–7000') usually with Oak, Juniper, and/or Pinyon as associates. It's more likely to be found in dappled shady places like gulches, canyon bottoms (sides), and next to intermittent drainages rather than in exposed areas.

Edible Uses
Begin to look for Pinyon ricegrass' seed panicles in early August. Wait for their full development, then with thumb and forefinger, pull the entire panicle from the grass.

    Set the seed panicles aside for 1–2 weeks so they dry completely. Rub/roll the seed panicles vigorously together between hands. This separates the seed from the stems. With just the seed, repeat this process several more times. Once most of the chaff has been separated, winnow the seed in a light breeze or fan set on low.

    The processed seed is good for four and meal purposes, rather than as a raw snack or seed sprinkle (some chaff remains after hand processing).

Medicinal Uses, Cautions, & Special Note
There are no medicinal uses or cautions for Pinyon ricegrass. There is little to no ethnobotanical information on the utilization of Pinyon ricegrass for food. However, the grass is fairly common throughout the Chiricahua Apache's traditional territory (photos were taken in the Chiricahuas). It's my opinion that this grain was locally utilized but has not been reported/ recorded due to information/communication loss.

Sustenance Index: High
Pictured: *Piptochaetium fimbriatum*

Salsify
Tragopogon dubius

Other Common Names
Yellow salsify, Goat's beard, Oyster root

Range & Habitat
Tragopogon dubius is the main Salsify species found throughout the state. The plant is non–native, biannual/short–lived perennial, and widespread.

Typically found at mid to high elevations, look for it on grassy areas that have at one time been disturbed – lawn and park edges, trailsides, embankments, etc.

Edible Uses
The upper parts (flower, leaf, and stem) are picked and eaten raw, or steamed/sautéed as a cooked green. A good–tasting and mild plant, these parts are non–bitter and very palatable. Try to collect the foliage before the flower goes to seed. It is more tender at this point.

Salsify roots can be eaten raw, but most find them better if first boiled/steamed/sautéed. They are mildly bitter–tasting and provide more complex carbohydrates than the upper parts. The roots of older plants tend to be a little more fibrous and bitter, especially if in their second or third year.

Medicinal Uses & Cautions
There are no significant medicinal uses or cautions for Salsify.

Special Note
All parts of the plant exude a milky latex if cut or torn. Another identifying feature is its large softball–sized seed puff–ball.

Sustenance Index: Medium
Pictured: *Tragopogon dubius*

44

Salt Bush
Atriplex spp.

Other Common Names
Saltweed, Shadscale, Desert holly, Quail bush

Range & Habitat
Salt bush is primarily a western US shrub, common to alkaline/saline soils. Look to low to middle elevations: flats, alluvial fans, bottomlands, and dirt roadsides. Nearly two dozen perennial species are listed for Arizona.

Edible Uses
The discussion that follows is for the perennial species of Atriplex (with salty–tasting leaves). For annual species, see Tumbling orache (page 54).

Most shrub species of Atriplex are called Salt bush due to their leaf–surface sodium deposition. Although a number of perennial species do have alleged edible uses (i.e. Four–wing salt bush), I've found their palatability so poor, that I consider them only for salt collection, and little else. I have not sampled all species of Salt bush, so there are likely exceptions to this observation.

A quick soak (do not simmer) of the fresh leaves in water makes a nice salt–water solution. Use it as an electrolyte drink (mainly sodium) or as a broth/brine base.

Medicinal Uses, Cautions, & Special Note
Medicinal uses for this family (Amaranth) are insignificant. Due to the plant's oxalate content, or another factor, Salt bush (leaves and seeds) can be irritating to the mouth/throat when eaten fresh. Additionally, many species stink (and lather) when boiled (for instance, Quail bush). Relatedly, a few species were used as a hair conditioner/shampoo. Generally, the larger–leaved and annual species are better for food uses. Tasting is believing: try a fresh leaf of whatever species. If non–acrid/non–bitter, then it will be a good cooked green/seed provider.

Sustenance Index: Low

Pictured: *Atriplex polycarpa (top)* | *Atriplex lentiformis (bottom)*

Serviceberry

Amelanchier alnifolia and A. utahensis

Other Common Names
Alder–leaf serviceberry, Utah serviceberry

Range & Habitat
Of the two species of Serviceberry found in Arizona, Utah serviceberry is by far the most common. It is abundant from the White Mountains and Mogollon Rim to the San Francisco Peaks and Kaibab Plateau. Pinyon and Ponderosa pine elevations are its preferred associations.

At similar elevations, Alder–leaf serviceberry is found from the Flagstaff area to the north side of the Grand Canyon. The plant is at the edge of it range here; it is primarily a Rocky Mountain and Pacific–state shrub.

Edible Uses
Ripening mid to late summer, the purple fruit are eaten raw. Though seed–filled, if found in optimal condition, they are sweet and juicy. If discovered early, late, or environmentally stressed, the fruit is often dry and mealy, and is a better candidate for a jelly preparation.

Medicinal Uses
Like many Rose family plants, Serviceberry leaves are mildly astringent. Use the leaf tea as a wash for bruises, stings, and insect bites.

Cautions
Serviceberry seeds, like most from the Rose family, contain traces of cyanogenic glycosides. Drying/grinding/heating destroys these compounds. But even fresh in small to moderate quantities, there is little to fear from the seed. There are no cautions for the fleshy portion of the fruit.

Sustenance Index: Medium

Pictured: *Amelanchier alnifolia (top)* | *A. utahensis (bottom)* | *A. spp. (circle)*

46

Sheep's Sorrel
Rumex acetosella

Other Common Names
Field sorrel, Red sorrel

Range & Habitat
This non–native herbaceous perennial is somewhat common to higher
elevations (5500'–8500') throughout
Arizona. Preferring disturbed soils,
look for it next to trails, ditches, and
minimally–traveled dirt roadsides in
full sun exposures.

Edible Uses
Sheep's sorrel is best utilized as a
fresh herb in salads or as a garnish.
The leaves being the main edible part,
are tangy and sour–tasting (oxalates).
Moderate amounts can be consumed
raw; however, if eating more than a
hand–full, I recommend first giving
the leaves a quick boil and rinse. This
will diminish some of the leaves' oxalate content.

Medicinal Uses
Sheep's sorrel is not particularly medicinal; however, the plant's therapeutic void has not stopped product
hucksters from promoting it as part
of a 'cancer–cure' herbal combination.

Cautions
Excess consumption of oxalates may lead
to urinary tract irritation and stone development (if prone to their formation). Boil-
ing/rinsing Sheep's sorrel reduces its oxalate concentration.

Special Note
Two characteristics will help in identifying Sheep's sorrel: 1) sour taste; 2) the leaves are ar-
row–shaped with pointed base lobes (hastate). Although unrelated, Sheep's sorrel and Sorrel (Oxalis) are identical in edible use (foliage).

Sustenance Index: Low
Pictured: *Rumex acetosella*

Smartweed
Persicaria spp.

Other Common Names
Lady's thumb, Knotweed

Range & Habitat
Arizona hosts a handful of Persicaria species, the majority of which are native. Persicaria maculosa (Spotted lady's thumb) is the most widespread introduced species. Almost all bodies of water in Arizona, up to about 9000', have at least one species of Smartweed thriving on its banks; look to the sides of perennial rivers, ponds, lakes, and ciénegas.

Edible Uses
Gather the just–emerging young leaves and tender stems, preferably before the plant flowers. In small amounts they can be chopped and eaten fresh as a salad ingredient. Larger quantities are consumed as a boiled green. With a little seasoning, they make a fine–tasting, spinach/chard–like wild vegetable.

Medicinal Uses
Not commonly used today, Smartweed species were employed by various Indian tribes for an array of minor issues. Interestingly, there is some application similarity between Persicaria and Rumex (Yellowdock). Both plants belong to the same family and are chemically affiliated.

Cautions & Special Note
Water contamination and harmful waterborne microorganisms are likely the greatest concern when utilizing Smartweed. Make sure to give the leaves a clean water rinse (or boil) prior to consuming.

One feature that helps to identify several Smartweed species is a notable mid–leaf purple spot (like a lady's partial thumb print).

Sustenance Index: Low
Pictured: *Persicaria spp.*

Sorrel
Oxalis spp.

Other Common Names
Alpine woodsorrel, Tenleaf woodsorrel, Sourgrass

Range & Habitat
The two main higher elevation Sorrel species (purple–pink flowers) in Arizona are Oxalis decaphylla (Tenleaf woodsorrel) and O. alpina (Alpine woodsorrel). Both are found at 5000'–9500' elevations. Look to Ponderosa pine shady areas, usually next to rocks. From Flagstaff and the Mogollon Rim area, to the White Mountains and the state's southeastern mountain chains, the two plants are fairly common.

Yellow–flowering sorrels grow lower in elevation and do not have bulb roots. These species are fine for foliage uses.

Edible Uses
The leaves, flowers, and green seed pods of all Sorrel species are edible. They are best eaten raw (in small to moderate amounts), added to salads or used as a sandwich garnish for their tart–sour taste. For the consumption of large amounts, the foliage is best boiled/steamed.

Oxalis decaphylla and O. alpina have pea–sized bulb–type roots. They are carbohydrate rich and have a crisp and pleasantly bland taste. They are fine eaten fresh or cooked.

Medicinal Uses
There are no medicinal uses for Sorrel.

Cautions
Sorrel contains oxalates. Excessive leaf consumption (as a big salad every day) could potentially lead to kidney irritation/stone formation if prone to these problems. There are no cautions for the bulb, the leaf as an occasional edible, or larger amounts of the leaf if first boiled and rinsed.

Sustenance Index: Medium
Pictured: *Oxalis alpina (top & bottom) | Oxalis decaphylla (circle)*

Spectacle Fruit
Wislizenia refracta (Wislizenia costellata)

Other Common Names
Jackass clover

Range & Habitat
Found throughout Arizona, look for Spectacle fruit at an array of elevations: 1000'–8000'. But really, the most abundant populations are found in the middle range. The plant prefers the sandy soils of wash sides, roadsides, and even the disturbed soils of vacant lots. It's a quick responder to monsoon rains and is easily mistaken for a large flowering Mustard during this time.

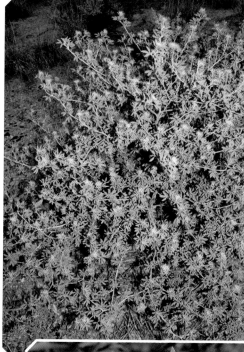

Edible Uses
Like Beeplant and Jones' beeplant, Spectacle fruit is an edible Mustard–like green. Consumed fresh (leaf–flower–fruit) it is pungent–spicy, necessitating its judicious use. Employ it in limited amounts as a salad addition or sandwich garnish. Briefly steamed or sautéed, larger amounts can be eaten; heat dissipates Spectacle fruit's volatile Mustard oil, making the plant's consumption not only possible, but enjoyable. Unlike Beeplant and Jones' beeplant, Spectacle fruit's early–green pods (eyeglass shaped) are too small to be utilized like capers – just include them with the leaf/flower as part of the fresh/cooked green.

Medicinal Uses, Cautions, & Special Note
Aside from a small handful of the fresh herb being useful for indigestion (not heartburn), there are no important medicinal uses for the plant. Too much fresh material will likely upset the stomach, irritate the mouth/throat, and possibly stimulate menses (a common side–effect of Mustard oils). Spectacle fruit belongs to the Beeplant family (Cleomaceae). Most members are fast–growing annuals (or herbaceous perennials). This family is related to the Mustard family (Brassicaceae); members of both families often share culinary characteristics.

Sustenance Index: Low
Pictured: *Wislizenia refracta*

Spiderwort

Tradescantia occidentalis and T. pinetorum

Other Common Names
Prairie spiderwort, Western spiderwort, Pinewoods spiderwort

Range & Habitat
Two species of Spiderwort are common in Arizona. Tradescantia occidentalis is found at middle elevations, mostly on rocky slopes and in grassland areas. T. pinetorum grows at higher Pine forest elevations. Both plants prefer full–sun exposures.

Edible Uses
All parts of Spiderwort are edible, either fresh or cooked. Needing no preparation, the entire above–ground young plant (flower, stem, and leaf) is simply picked when encountered and eaten raw. Some parts may be a little fibrous, but nevertheless, the plant is pleasant tasting.

The roots (marble–sized tubers for Tradescantia pinetorum; slender but thickened roots for T. occidentalis) are mild and semi–starchy (sometimes a little fibrous). Eat them raw or better yet, chop, simmer, and season as a cooked vegetable. Bland–tasting, they are fine consumed solo, or in combination with other edibles.

Medicinal Uses & Cautions
There are no medicinal uses or cautions for Spiderwort.

Special Note
Spiderwort is botanically related to Day-flower (same family – Commelinaceae). Both plants have identical edible uses and should be considered interchangeable. The ornamental species of Spiderwort (Wandering Jew – Tradescantia fluminensis and T. zebrina), grown as a ground cover in warmer parts of the country, are also edible. The young fleshy leaves are best chopped and used as a salad ingredient.

Sustenance Index: Medium
Pictured: *Tradescantia occidentalis (top & bottom)* | *Tradescantia pinetorum (circle)*

Springparsley
Cymopterus spp.

Other Common Names
Wild parsnip, Chimaja

Range & Habitat
Cymopterus glomeratus, C. purpu-rascens, and C. multinervatus are the three main Arizona species of Springparsley. All are found at about 3000′/4000′–7000′. C. glomeratus is a northeastern Arizona grower. It's common to sandy–rocky soils. C. purpurascens is found throughout northern parts of the state. C. mult-inervatus, the commonest species, is found nearly state–wide. Look for Springparsley on mountain foothills – typically in association with grass-land/scrub vegetation.

Edible Uses
The roots of Springparsley are its main edible part. Taking on a stor-age/tap root orientation, they reach depths of 1′–2′ (the dry and rocky soils in which they are found makes for dif-ficult digging). Parsnip–like, mild, and not too fibrous, they are fine eaten either raw, or more so, if first cooked. They're a good carbohydrate source.

    The foliage and seeds tend to be mildly bitter and/or aromatic...edible, however, best is first simmered and rinsed.

Medicinal Uses, Cautions, & Special Note
Cymopterus glomeratus (Chimaja), is the best–known spice–medicinal species. Its leaves are used as a cilantro–like garnish; the seeds, as a mild spice–carminative.

There are no cautions for Springparsley. It's worth mentioning too, that Cymopterus is called Springparsley for good reason. April to May is the plant's above–ground window. It emerg-es, flowers, and sets seed all in about 3–4 weeks; after which, every trace of the plant van-ishes until next year. All belonging to the Carrot family, the roots of Springparsley, Mountain parsley, and Biscuitroot can be treated about the same in terms of edibility.

Sustenance Index: Medium
Pictured: *Cymopterus multinervatus*

Thimbleberry
Rubus parviflorus

Other Common Names
Western thimbleberry

Range & Habitat
Thimbleberry's main territory consti-
tutes the Rocky Mountains and higher mountains of the Pacific states.

   In Arizona, it is most reliably
found throughout the White Mountains. Additional stands are also located in the higher elevations of the
Chuska, Pinaleño, and Chiricahua
Mountains. Look for the plant in dappled shade from Aspen and conifers.

Edible Uses
Ripening mid to late summer, Thimbleberry's fruit tastes similar to Raspberry, yet not quite as succulent. They
are fine eaten fresh – the drupelets
peeled away from the drupe core.
They too can be dried for future use
or prepared as a jam/jelly.

   Thimbleberry is like Raspberry in nutritional aspects. It contains
good amounts of vitamin C, potassium, and magnesium.

Medicinal Uses
Like New Mexico raspberry, Thimbleberry leaf is used as a Raspberry leaf
replacement. Drink the tea as urinary tract
soother and female reproductive astringent.

Cautions
There are no cautions for Thimbleberry.

Special Note
Thimbleberry in Arizona tends to be smaller in size than plants growing in more northernly
latitudes. Fruit production too is often more sporadic and smaller than Rocky Mountain and
Pacific Northwest plants. Arizona Dewberry, Blackberry, New Mexico raspberry, Raspberry,
and Thimbleberry are all closely related.

Sustenance Index: Medium
Pictured: *Rubus parviflorus*

Tumbling Orache

Atriplex rosea

Other Common Names
Tumbling saltweed, Redscale salt bush

Range & Habitat
An annual indigenous to Eurasia, Tumbling orache is an occasionally encountered weed. Almost always found in disturbed soils, look for it in ditches, next to culverts, edges of secondary roadsides, etc. It germinates and grows quickly in response to monsoon rains. It's mainly found in northern Arizona – around Flagstaff, the Kaibab Plateau, and Navajo/Hopi Reservations.

Edible Uses
Related to Amaranth and Lambsquarters, botanically and in use, consider Tumbling orache a low–level edible cooked green. The young leaves are gathered early–mid August and simmered/rinsed and consumed as a spinach–like vegetable. The cooking process is important for the leaves; fresh, they are poor–tasting (not terrible, but not good either). I've yet to sample the seeds, but it is said they are somewhat edible and similar to what Lambsquarters' provides.

Medicinal Uses & Cautions
There are no medicinal uses for Tumbling orache. The plant likely harbors moderate to high levels of oxalates – just be sure to simmer/rinse the leaves before eating.

Special Note
Tumbling orache is closely related to Salt bush (page 45); however, Tumbling orache is not particularly salty. Even though the plant has only been in America for two to three hundred years, the Navajo are reported to have used it as an edible in times of scarcity (leaves and seeds) and as a livestock fodder.

Sustenance Index: Low
Pictured: *Atriplex rosea*

Utah Honeysuckle

Lonicera utahensis

Other Common Names
Red twinberry, Fly honeysuckle

Range & Habitat
Principally a plant of the Middle and Northern Rockies, in Arizona, Utah honeysuckle is found almost exclusively in the White Mountains. Here, it's an occasional sub–shrub preferring dappled shade areas next to streams and drainages (9500'–11000').

Edible Uses
The red berries are juicy and semi–sweet – not at all bad tasting. Eat them fresh (insignificant seeds) as a trail snack or dry them for later as an addition to other dried fruit and nuts. If enough of the fruit is available, they also make a fine jelly/preserve base.

Medicinal Uses
The flowers and leaves are similar in use to Japanese honeysuckle (*Lonicera japonica*): use the infusion as a mild antiviral diaphoretic during cold and flu season. Most Lonicera species can be used this way and are related to Elder (same family) in application.

Cautions
There are no cautions for the fruit.

Special Note
There are a handful of native Honeysuckle species in Arizona, with most having inedible fruit (not poisonous per se, but very poor tasting). The only other species to be encountered in the White Mountains, at similar elevations, is Lonicera involucrata (Twinberry). It's a large shrub with non–edible bitter–tasting black berries. Arizona honeysuckle (Lonicera arizonica) grows below 9500'. Its leaves are more ovate than Utah honeysuckle's. Also, Utah honeysuckle's berries form in pairs (obscured by leaves in the photo); Arizona honeysuckle's berries are also red but multi–clustered. I've never sampled Arizona honeysuckle's berries, but it's said they are bitter.

Sustenance Index: Medium
Pictured: *Lonicera utahensis*

Wild Grape

Vitis arizonica

Other Common Names
Arizona grape, Canyon grape

Range & Habitat
Common throughout the state, look for Wild grape along canyon bottoms and next to streams and intermittent drainages. Sometimes found at desert elevations (next to water), Wild grape is more predictably encountered in middle zones: 4000'–7000'. Above average soil hydration is important for its existence and like most vines, it will be found growing up through and over support shrubs/trees.

Edible Uses
Wild grape falls into two categories: plants that produce edible fruit and ones that produce non–edible fruit. I believe soil hydration and elevation are two important factors when evaluating Wild grape's edibility. Lower–elevation/drier–growing Wild grapes usually produce fruits that are acrid. If eaten fresh, they will irritate the mouth and throat; not dangerous, but annoying. Drying–heating diminishes these factors. Better–tasting plants are usually found higher in elevation and/or in soils with greater hydration. Here, the fruit will be sweet and Juicy (but still seed filled) and are fine eaten raw or prepared as a jelly. Not a significant food, the curling tendrils that grasp close–by plants (or trellises) are tart tasting. The young leaves can be prepared like cultivated grape leaves; however, they become less edible with age.

Medicinal Uses, Cautions, & Special Note
Aside from antioxidants found within the fruit's skin and seeds, there are no major medicinal uses for Wild grape. It is interesting to note though, Wild grape's acrid principles too seem to be confined to mainly the skin and seeds.

Sustenance Index: Medium
Pictured: *Vitis arizonica*

Wild Onion
Allium spp.

Other Common Names
Nodding onion, Geyer's onion, Twincrest onion

Range & Habitat
The two abundant species of Wild onion in Arizona are Allium cernuum (Nodding onion) and A. geyeri (Geyer's onion). Common to conifer–Aspen elevations, these plants are found from the Navajo Reservation and Flagstaff to the Mogollon Rim and White Mountains. A number of species are additionally found in the Sky Islands of southeastern Arizona.

Edible Uses
All Wild onion species can be distinguished from other monocots by their distinctive onion scent. The entire plant – leaf, flower stalk (scape), flowers, and bulb are equally edible. The bulb has the strongest flavor; the herbaceous portions – the mildest.

All parts can be eaten fresh (limited); however, for the consumption of larger amounts (bulb), it should first be cooked/baked. This will remove much of the bulb's harshness. Wrapped in foil with a bouillon cube and then set on campfire coals for 10–15 minutes is a fine way to proceed.

Medicinal Uses, Cautions, & Special Note
In terms of medicinal strength, Wild onion can be thought of as a diminutive Garlic (another Allium). A Wild onion honey steep makes a serviceable cold and flu application. It will be found mildly antibacterial and antiviral. Too much raw Wild onion will cause digestive upset.

If it looks like a Wild onion, yet has no onion smell, unless properly identified as another edible plant, then do not eat it. The plant is not Wild onion, but likely another related plant – some of which are edible, but some too are toxic (for instance, Deathcamas).

Sustenance Index: Medium
Pictured: *Allium cernuum (top & circle)* | *Allium acuminatum (bottom)*

Wild Potato

Solanum jamesii

Other Common Names

James' wild potato, Indian potato

Range & Habitat

Mainly an Arizona–New Mexico plant, Wild potato is most prolific from the northern part of the state to the San Francisco Peaks, Mogollon Rim, and White Mountains. Outlier populations can be found in the Huachuca and Chiricahua Mountains.

From 5000'–8500', look for it in dappled shade areas in association with Ponderosa pine, Pinyon pine, and Oak.

Edible Uses

Botanically allied with common potato (native to the Andes), Wild potato's tuber is the sought–after part. About the size of a small to large marble, they are located not far below the ground's surface. Once gathered and rinsed, be sure to simmer them for 20–30 minutes. This preparation is important. It serves to cook, but also reduces any potential alkaloid principle. Rinse, re–simmer (if still uncooked), and enjoy as a starchy carbohydrate–rich meal. The tuber's taste is the same as a regular potato, with a hint of bitter – not at all overpowering.

The Hopi, Navajo, and Apache (and other tribes) utilized Wild potato as a supplemental food, usually in times of crop/game scarcity.

Medicinal Uses & Cautions

The entire plant (tubers lesser so) likely harbors low levels of alkaloids common to most Solanum species. Medicinal uses for these plants tend to be as anticholinergics (lessening to GI, bronchial, and skin activity). Wild Solanum species are less toxic than Datura/Atropa/Hyoscyamus when medicinally used in excess; however, be attentive to heat flush sensations, mouth dryness, and dizziness if the foliage is ingested (tea or tincture).

Sustenance Index: Medium
Pictured: *Solanum jamesii*

Wild Rose
Rosa woodsii

Other Common Names
Woods' rose

Range & Habitat
A wide–ranging species, look for Wild rose between 5000'–9000'. Preferring the sides of intermittent drainages, it typically is found in full or partial sun exposures.

Most abundant in the northern/central mountains (San Francisco Peaks/Mogollon Rim/White Mountains), it too can be found throughout many of the southeastern Sky Islands.

Edible Uses
The fruit of Wild rose (any Rose species) is called a hip. Ripening late summer to early fall, they can be eaten fresh, but are not great tasting: seed–filled/insipid. Their best preparation will be as a jelly or syrup base. The hips' high vitamin content makes it an important forage if nutritional deficiency (especially vitamin C) is suspected. For this reason, the dried hips were an important cold–season food supplement, especially if the diet was limited (cabin shut–in: canned food/jerky/beans/etc.). Relatedly, crushed hips were a common a pemmican ingredient.

Medicinal Uses & Cautions
The encapsulated hip powder (or simply mixed with water), taken internally, is nutritional (vitamin C, minerals, and health–promoting lipids). It also is broadly antiinflammatory and tissue/skin supportive. The leaves are mildly astringent and used as a poultice on minor bites, stings, and burns. Wild rose is caution–free.

Special Note
Cultivated Roses are used the same way as Wild rose.

Sustenance Index: Medium
Pictured: *Rosa woodsii*

Wild Strawberry

Fragaria vesca and F. virginiana

Other Common Names
Woodland strawberry, Virginia strawberry

Range & Habitat
Range and habitat (and physical characteristics) for both plants are essentially interchangeable, with Fragaria virginiana being the more abundant of the two species.

From the Kaibab Plateau and San Francisco Peaks, to the Mogollon Rim, White Mountains, and Sky Islands, look to high elevations for Wild strawberry. It is most often found in dappled shade with Fir, Spruce, and/or Aspen overhead.

Edible Uses
The edibility of Wild strawberry needs little explanation; they are just as tasty as garden–grown or store–bought Strawberry (usually the cultivar – Fragaria X ananassa).

Eat the fruit fresh, dehydrated for later, or prepared as a jam/jelly or preserve. Like the cultivated type, Wild strawberry is high in potassium and contains fair amounts of vitamin C.

The drawbacks to Wild strawberry are its small fruit size and erratic fruit development. Plants lower in elevation are often sterile. The best fruit producers grow at about 9500' and higher.

Medicinal Uses
Wild strawberry leaf is mildly astringent. As a topically applied poultice, it is arresting and inflammation–reducing to minor cuts and scrapes. Internally, the leaf tea is used as a substitute for Raspberry leaf tea (female reproductive tonic).

Cautions
There are no cautions for Wild strawberry.

Sustenance Index: Medium
Pictured: *Fragaria virginiana*

Yampa

Perideridia parishii

Other Common Names
Parish's yampah

Range & Habitat
Associated with conifer elevations, look for Yampa between 6500'–10000'. It's almost always found in forest openings where the soil is hydrated: moist meadows and grassy–boggy stream sides. Yampa grows from the North Rim of the Grand Canyon and Coconino National Forest to the Mogollon Rim and White Mountains.

Edible Uses
The seed, flower, leaf, and stem are eaten raw; however, the small tubers are the sought–after part. They lie just below the ground's surface and are small: 1"–2" long by ½"–¾" wide, with 1–2 tubers per plant being the norm. They are pleasantly crunchy (not fibrous) eaten fresh. I can't seem to keep for eating them immediately, but I'm sure they too are a fine cooking candidate.

Medicinal Uses, Cautions, & Special Note
There are no medicinal uses or cautions (keep reading) for Yampa. The tubers can be difficult to collect due to their tendency of growing in thick–grassy areas; they are usually enmeshed within a network of fine grass roots. If the tubers do not look like what is pictured...do not eat them! It's possible you have collected the wrong (and poisonous) plant. Yampa is small (1'–2' high), very slender, delicate, with fine–parted spear–linear leaves (vein travels to the leaflet tip). Water Hemlock (deadly) is a larger plant, usually growing directly in water with large/coarse leaves (leaflet vein travels to the cut). Its roots are clustered and much larger than Yampa's. Poison hemlock (deadly) is too a large plant, but it has fern–like leaves, with a semi–woody taproot. Anyway – be sure the proper plant is being collected. Mistakes with Carrot family plants can be deadly.

Sustenance Index: High
Pictured: *Perideridia parishii*

Index